THE TROY STETINA SERIES

CW01022249

METAL LEAD GUITAR

PRIMER

ISBN 0-7935-1097-X

HAL•LEONARD®

7777 W. BLUEMOUND RD. P.O. BOX 13819 MILWAUKEE, WI 53213

ABOUT THE AUTHOR

Troy Stetina is internationally recognized as a leading authority in guitar instruction and a critically-acclaimed guitar virtuoso. His best-selling books, methods and videos have been applauded by the various guitar magazines and used by teachers and guitarists the world over. Troy has been a contributing writer for *Guitar World, Guitar School,* and *Guitar One* magazines, and he has also created programs for workshops as well as a university-level course for rock and metal guitar at the Wisconsin Conservatory of Music, where he was formerly Director of Rock Guitar Studies. A list of books and videos in the *Troy Stetina Series* appears at the end of this book.

WELCOME TO THE "TROY STETINA SERIES"

The *TROY STETINA SERIES* is a complete system for mastering metal and building solid musicianship. It covers the full spectrum of metal guitar, from the beginning up to a professional level of playing. And it is designed by someone who specializes in metal, so each method gives you just what you really need to get playing quickly and correctly. To help you select the right books, methods, and videos for your current playing level, see the brief descriptions at the end of this book.

FOREWORD

Metal Lead Guitar Primer is the beginner's entry-level introduction to the Metal Lead Guitar Method. It is designed to get you-the beginning guitarist-playing metal licks and solos as quickly as possible, while introducing you to fundamental musical concepts. Those already familiar with the concepts here may skip to *Metal Lead Guitar, Volume One.*

This *Primer* looks at rock scales, string damping, technique-building exercises, pulse and rhythm notation, key changes, and the basic guitar articulations. At the end of each chapter, the concepts are applied in a full-band jam, in which you trade, or echo, short solo phrases with a pre-recorded lead track.

Beginners are recommended to start *Metal Rhythm Guitar, Volume One* at the same time, as both work together to build a complete foundation for metal guitar. Additionally, you may find it helpful to supplement these books with the beginning videos of the series. A book/CD format is best for offering the most material and in-depth explanations, but video's offer something a book just can't do – an opportunity to actually see the techniques demonstrated live. So each has its own place in the scheme of things. And of course, the best situation is to use every tool to help you get where you want to go.

Good luck with your playing, and enjoy the method!

THE ELECTRIC GUITAR

For reference purposes, the parts of the electric guitar are labelled below (just in case you don't already know them). Of course not every design will correspond exactly to the following picture, but they will be similar.

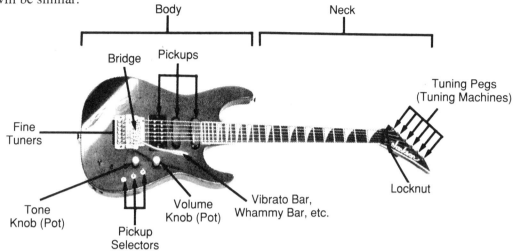

The parts of the electric guitar

When a string is stretched tight, it vibrates at a certain pitch. If the string is shortened, the pitch goes up. Likewise, notes (or pitches) may be played on the guitar by striking any open string. Higher notes may be played on a string by "fretting" it—that is, holding the string down firmly against the fretboard and thereby pressing it against one of the metal frets. This shortens the length of the string that can vibrate, so the pitch goes up. The higher you fret (press) on the neck, the more the effective length of the string is shortened, and the higher the pitch goes.

Underneath the strings on the body of the guitar you'll find the "pickups." They contain magnets, because when metal strings vibrate in a magnetic field, electrical impulses are created, transferring the acoustical energy (vibration) into electrical energy. The impulses travel from the guitar, through any "effects" devices, and then to an amplifier where the signal is amplified. Finally it is converted back to acoustical energy (sound) by the speakers.

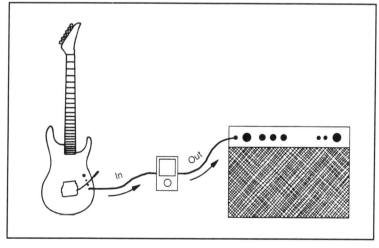

Basic setup

See "Getting the Sound," page 45, for more information on amps, guitars, and effects pedals.

3

POSITIONING

As you probably already know, a standing position is usually used for performance. For practice, a sitting position is less fatiguing, but if you only practice in a sitting position you will get comfortable playing in that position only. When you try to play standing up, it won't feel right because the angle of your arms and hands to the guitar is different. The lower you wear the guitar when you stand, the more different it will feel. Therefore, when you're starting out it's a good idea to practice at least half of the time standing up. Both positions should be equally comfortable.

Practice at least half the time standing up.

Electric guitar requires the opposite approach from that of acoustic guitar. On an acoustic guitar, the strings don't make noise unless they are caused to ring. With a loud, heavily-distorted electric guitar on the other hand, the strings will tend to "take off" on their own and make noise unless something is done to prevent this. (See "feedback," page 46.) Therefore, the resting position—when you aren't playing—is with your right and left hands lightly touching all six strings, to hold them quiet.

Make it a habit to hold the strings mute
with both hands when you aren't playing.

An important part of metal guitar technique is learning to always hold every string mute that is not intended to ring out, so that you don't have unwanted string noise interfering with the notes that you are playing. The position above is the first step—there will be more on this throughout the book.

There are basically two different positions for the left hand: one is with the thumb behind the neck, the other is with the thumb hooked over the top of the neck. With your thumb behind the neck, your fingers can get a wider stretch—particularly on the lower frets and lower sounding strings. The second position offers more strength and control for string bending and works well for pentatonic scales, which will be the focus of this book. However, you should be aware of both positions and be able to switch freely between them.

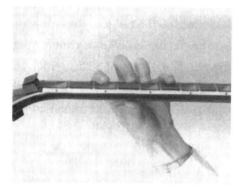

Thumb behind neck

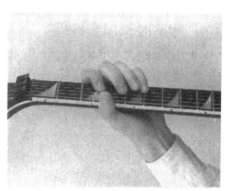

Thumb hooked over top

The standard way to hold the pick is between the thumb and first finger (as below). However, many guitarists hold the pick differently so there isn't any clearly "right" or "wrong" way.

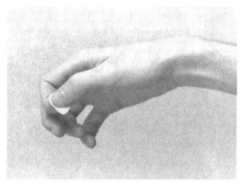

Holding the pick

Different right hand positions are also common, but they generally fit into three basic categories: Free-floating, anchored with the palm on the bridge-saddles, or anchored with the ring finger and little finger against the pickguard below the strings.

Free-floating right hand

Anchored with palm

Anchored with fingers

Use what feels natural, or copy the position used by players whose technique you would like to incorporate into your own. Most are available on videotape. I often use the second position because I use a lot of right hand muting. Other times I use the free-floating position.

STRINGS

I suggest using "extra light" gauge strings, commonly referred to as a set of "9's" based on the thickness of the first string. The actual string thicknesses of this gauge in thousands of an inch from the first to the sixth strings are: .009, .011, .016, .024, .032, and .042.

If you're doing a lot of string bending (and you will in this book), you will be breaking strings occasionally. Therefore, you should know how to replace them. First, thread the string through the bridge system like the rest of the strings on your guitar (different designs work differently) and thread it through the locking nut if your guitar is so equipped. Then, wind the string onto the tuning machines, but first stick it through the hole and twist it so that it won't slip. This is simple, but it can take a little practice. You might want to have someone show you how to do it the first time.

TUNING

It is important to keep your guitar in tune because every time you practice, you are also simultaneously developing your "ear" (your ability to discern pitch). Playing an out-of-tune guitar retards this development—not to mention that it sounds terrible! There are several different ways to tune.

For working in this book, you can use the tuning notes given at the beginning of the CD or cassette. Listen to each string and simply adjust the pitch up or down with the tuning machines on the headstock until each string sounds the same as that on the tape. If you don't get it the first time through, just repeat it as many times as necessary. (For those of you with locking systems, make sure you are unlocked before tuning, or use the fine tuners.)

Another way to tune up is to use an electronic tuner. This is probably the most accurate method. On the recording, my guitar was tuned to concert pitch (A=440) so this method will work, provided that you aren't using a tape deck that runs too fast or too slow.

If your guitar has a vibrato system you will probably have some trouble. In most designs, the tension of all the strings is balanced by a set of springs in the vibrato system. This is great because it enables you to pull up on the bar as well as push down, but it comes at a price. And the price is that tuning is more difficult. For example, suppose the strings on your guitar are a little flat (too low) and you raise the first string to pitch, then the second, third, fourth, etc. As you tune up each successive string, the bridge moves slightly, lowering the pitch of all the other strings. When you finish, the strings are still flat.

There are a couple of ways you can deal with this. One way is to tune over and over until the bridge stops moving so much. A more efficient method would be to anticipate the rise or drop in pitch, and tune on past the correct pitch approximately the right amount. With some practice, you can get it tuned in two passes. The only other options are to tighten the springs on the back of the vibrato system so that the bridge doesn't float, or buy a different guitar!

READING MUSIC IN THIS BOOK

This book uses tablature (TAB) because its the easiest and quickest way to learn how to play guitar. Learning to read standard notation, or staff, is also a very important skill and if you really want to take your music as far as you can, you should learn staff. However, that is beyond the scope of this book.

Tablature is a system of reading music that describes notes by giving the string and fret number which is to be played.

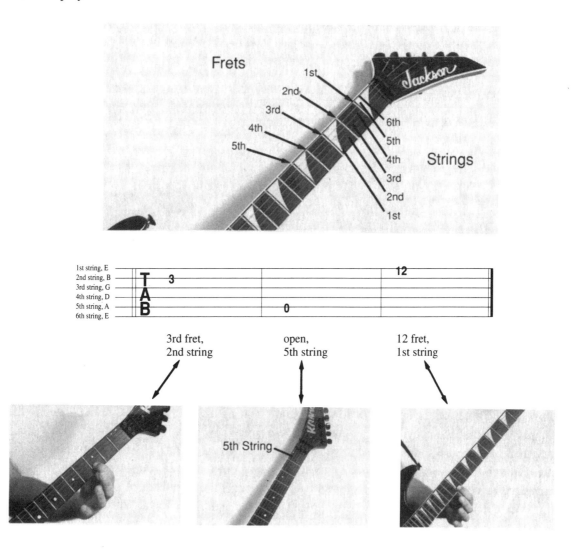

The fingers of the left hand are numbered:
- index finger - 1
- middle finger - 2
- ring finger   - 3
- little finger - 4

These fingering numbers appear below each tab line and tell you which left hand finger you should use to play a note.

The tablature system described above denotes the pitches of notes, where they are to be found on the neck of the guitar, and what finger to use. However, there is another aspect of musical notes that is just as important, and that is the *time value* of the notes—*when* to play them and *how long* they last. This aspect is described by *rhythm notation*, which will be introduced in Chapter Two. Until then, just copy the rhythms "by ear" from the examples on the cassette or CD.

CHAPTER ONE

Notes on the Low E String

The names of the notes on the low E string will be shown below on a fretboard diagram. To read a fretboard diagram, just imagine that you are looking down at a picture of the neck of the guitar, with the headstock to the left and the body of the guitar to the right. The fret numbers below the diagram correspond to the dots on the neck of the guitar.

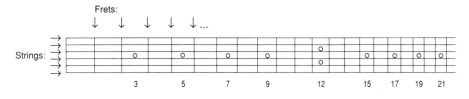

Below are the notes on the sixth, or lowest-sounding string up to the 12th fret. First, listen to the example on the accompanying cassette or CD so you know what it should sound like. (Each numbered example is demonstrated so you can make sure you are doing it right.) As you play up and down through the notes in example 1, say their names out loud until you think you've got them memorized reasonably well. The symbol " ⊓ " above each note indicates to pick the appropriate string with a *downstroke*. (A downstroke means that the pick moves toward the floor.)

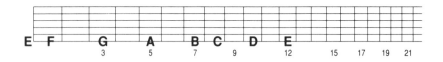

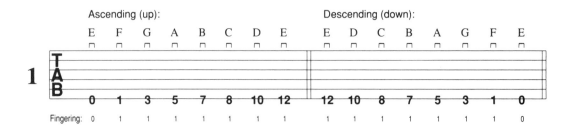

Starting at the 12th fret, the notes repeat one octave higher. The 12th fret is another "E," one octave above the open string (or "zero" fret); the 13th fret is "F," one octave above the 1st fret, etc. Notice that the dot pattern on the neck also repeats—that is, frets 15, 17, 19 and 21 follow the same pattern as 3, 5, 7 and 9. Also, although the fretboard diagram below shows 22 frets, 21 and 24 fret necks are common. The 24th fret is another "E" two octaves above the open string.

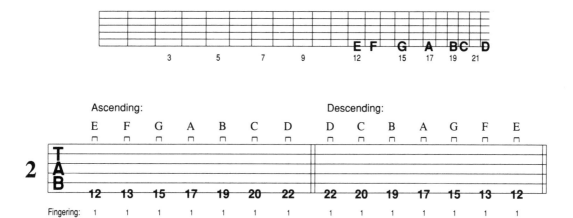

Now to test yourself, play the notes in the following fretboard diagrams, name them from memory and write them in the spaces to the right. The answers are below—no cheating!

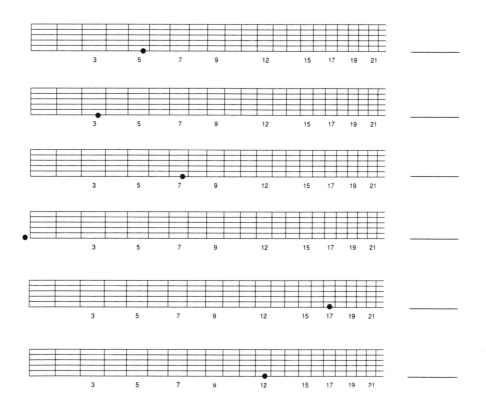

Answers: A: G; B; E; A; E

Keeping Non-Ringing Strings Quiet

A large part of metal guitar technique comes down to quieting, or muting, the strings that you don't want to ring. Otherwise, when you're playing with the amp turned up loud, those extra strings will be a constant headache for you, always adding unwanted noise. And how else are you going to keep them quiet when you're doing backflips off the drum riser? It may seem difficult now, but don't give up! You need to adopt this habit for everything you play.

The first step of this technique is to mute strings 1-5 when you are playing notes on the sixth string, as in the examples 1 and 2. Lay your first finger *lightly* across all six strings to hold them mute. Don't press down or you'll be fretting the strings. Instead, press only on the sixth string to fret the note you want, as in the diagram below. With this position, even if you accidentally pick another string it can't ring.

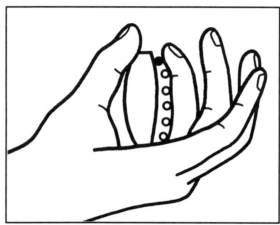

Playing notes on the 6th string

Test your muting in example 3. While each note is still ringing, intentionally pick the other strings—you should only hear the click of the pick striking the strings. If you hear anything else, you aren't muting the strings correctly. Fix it!

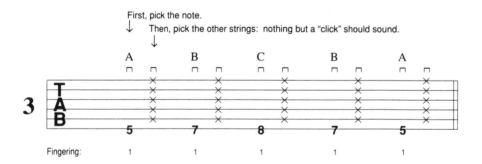

Now go back and play through examples 1 and 2 on the previous pages, but this time practice muting strings 1-5.

When you play notes on the other strings, you'll need to hold quiet both the higher sounding strings as well as the lower sounding strings. Use the side of your first finger for any higher strings as before. For the lower sounding strings, you will need to use the following techniques.

The tip of your first finger can always touch and hold the next lower string mute. When you are playing notes on the fifth string, use this technique to keep the sixth string quiet as in the diagram to the right.

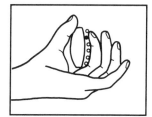

Playing on the 5th String

When you play notes on the fourth string, your first finger can mute strings 1-3 and string 5 using the above techniques. In addition, hook your thumb over the top of the neck to mute the sixth string as in the diagram.

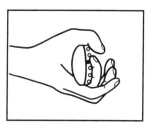

Playing on the 4th String

When you play notes on the first, second or third strings, some of the lower strings can't easily be muted with the left hand. Instead, try using your right hand palm to hold them quiet, if necessary.

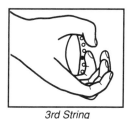

3rd String

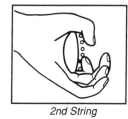

2nd String

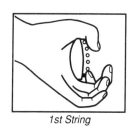

1st String

If you are doing this right, you should be able to strum across all the strings, yet only the right one will ring in example 4.

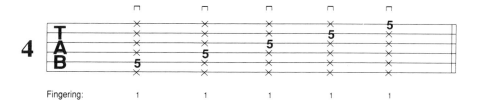

Keep in mind that while this is a good system for controlling the strings, it's not written in stone—different players may do it a little differently. You'll have to decide whether you want to do it my way or be stubborn and wrongheaded and follow your own sick preferences. That's OK, as long as you find *some* way to do it!

The Basic "Rock" Scale

A scale is a particular arrangement of notes that span an octave. In our current system of music theory, there are two types of scales that have priority status: major and minor. They are essentially opposites. Major sounds bright, happy, triumphant and uplifting. Minor sounds mournful, heavy and dark, or sometimes intense and dramatic—the evil designs of the predator stalking his next victim. (You've all seen the movies.) No one knows why we tend to associate opposite emotions with these scales, but we do.

The "minor pentatonic" scale is a special type of minor scale that has only five notes per octave instead of the usual seven tones. ("Penta" means five, and "tonic" refers to tones, or notes.) It is used at least to some extent by virtually every rock and metal player—from Chuck Berry to Kirk Hammet. Since the minor pentatonic scale below is based on an "A" note, it is called an "A minor pentatonic" scale. The A's are known as the *root* of the scale and are shown as squares in the fretboard diagram.

A Minor Pentatonic, 1st Octave

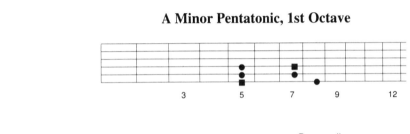

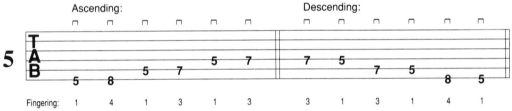

The next octave of the "A" minor pentatonic scale uses the same notes, just one octave higher. On the guitar, however, the pattern looks different. As you play, make sure that you keep all the strings that you don't want to sound muted.

A Minor Pentatonic, 2nd Octave

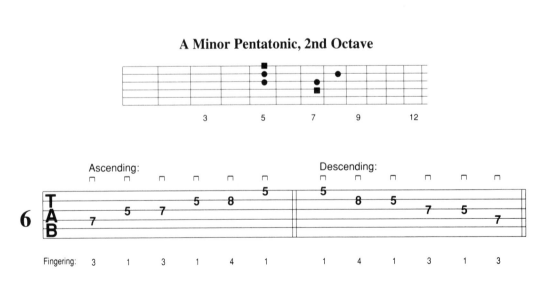

When both octaves are combined and one additional note is added above the highest root note, the position is completed. Memorize it!!! This is the most commonly used position for the pentatonic scale. Sometimes it's called a pentatonic "box" because of its two-note-per-string shape.

The A Minor Pentatonic "Box"

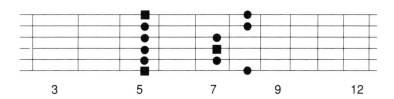

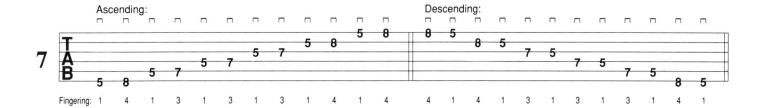

The pattern is repeated twelve frets higher. This is sometimes called the "octave position" of the pentatonic "box," since all of the notes are up one octave. Because the frets get smaller as you go higher on the neck, the same three fret stretch is actually much shorter. Therefore it is common to play the notes on the first and second strings with the fingering 1, 3 instead of 1, 4. (Keep in mind that fingerings aren't strict laws to be meticulously enforced. There are many exceptions and different ways to do things.)

The "Octave Position"

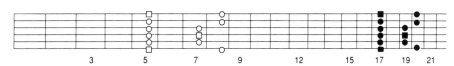

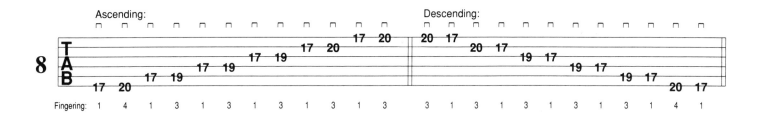

You'd be amazed at how many different sounds and styles can be squeezed out of this one scale. Listen to Eddie Van Halen's and Stevie Ray Vaughan's playing, for example. They both draw heavily from this same scale, yet they sound completely different!

Hammer-Ons and Pull-Offs

Notes are often played without picking the string, by using hammers and pulls. As the name suggests, a *hammer-on* means that the note is sounded by hammering your finger down. In the example below, pick the first note, then hammer your third finger down on the string to sound the second note. The whole time, your first finger should stay anchored, doing its job to hold the adjacent strings quiet.

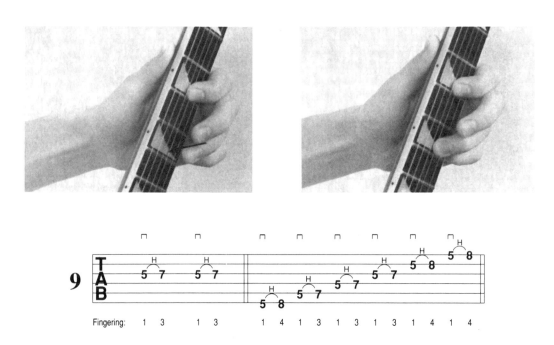

A *pull-off* is the opposite of a hammer-on. Pull your third finger down and off of the string to pluck it. Your first finger should be in place before you do the pull-off, and of course, it should be holding the adjacent strings mute. (If you hear any extra string noise, you aren't muting right—fix it!)

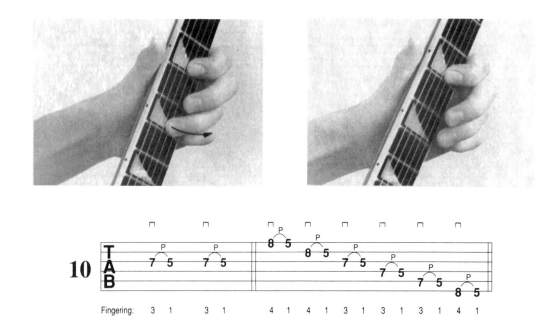

Get out your metronome for the following hammer/pull exercises. (If you don't already have a metronome, now's the time to get one.) Each example is played at two speeds: very slow, with the metronome set at 80 beats per minute (bpm), and a little faster, with the metronome ticking along at 120. Your first finger should remain anchored down on the fretboard throughout examples 11 and 12. The symbol ⁝ǁ at the end of each line means to repeat the line from the beginning. Make them sound just like they do on the cassette/CD.

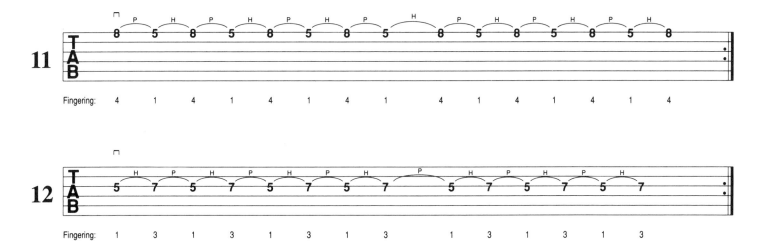

When you change strings, don't try to anchor your first finger *before* you play the first note on the next string, or you will always have a pause between notes as you change strings. That's a common mistake that people make. Instead, lead to the new string with the finger that will play the first note on that string (finger 3 or 4 in the examples below). Right after you pick that note on the new string, but before you do the pull-off, put your first finger in place and leave it anchored until it's time to change to another string.

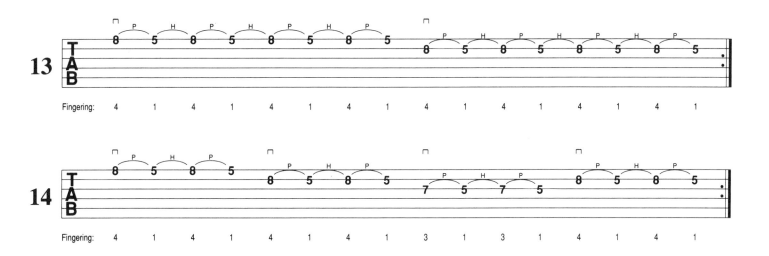

If you've done your homework on string muting, now you'll really start to notice some payoff— these exercises will sound clear without too much trouble. On the other hand, if you don't have the proper muting technique, your hammers, pulls and string changes will sound messy. If that's the case, figure out what is ringing and stop it. It won't go away until you make it go away.

The following hammer/pull exercises are written in the low "A" position, but practice them in the octave position as well. Again, each example is played at two speeds, with the metronome set at 80 and 120 bpm (in both low and high positions). Practice at various speeds, but keep in mind that at this point it's more important to play the notes evenly—particularly when you change between strings—than to burn up the fretboard.

Also, notice that the fingering is different on the first two strings, requiring an extra stretch for your third finger instead of using your fourth finger. The fingering you use depends on what you are playing. Since most of the licks in this book will favor using your third finger, this will be the focus for now. Later, when you get into scale-oriented runs, you will start using the fourth finger more.

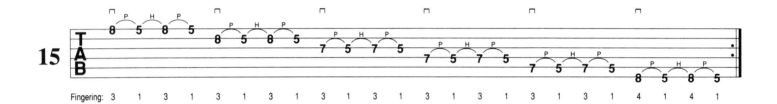

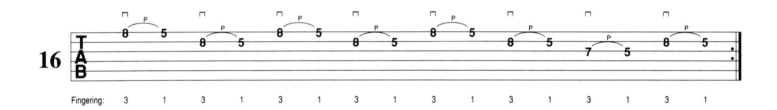

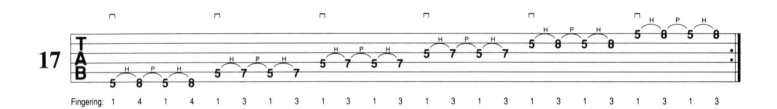

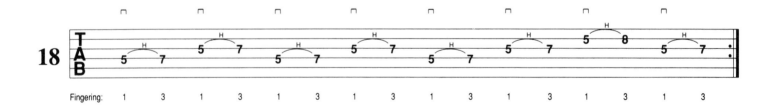

Although the metronome is slower in these examples, the notes are actually faster because more notes are played in the space of each beat. (You see, in the previous examples there were two notes to each beat. Below, there are four notes per beat in examples 19 and 20, and three notes per beat in examples 21 and 22.) Slow down the metronome a little. As long as you keep the notes even and there is no unwanted string noise, you can slowly increase your speed. Again, play each example in both the low position, as written, and up in the octave position.

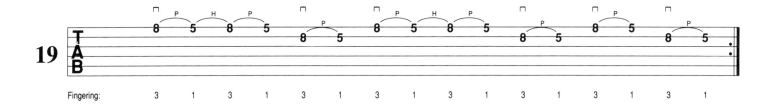

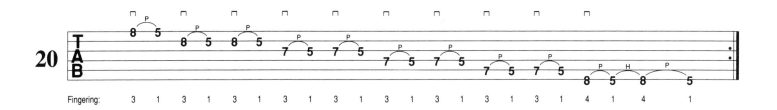

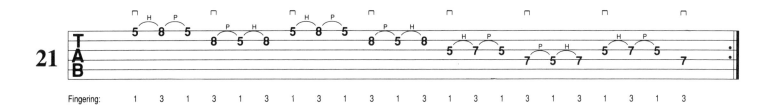

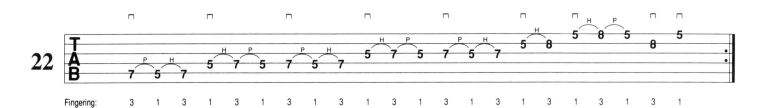

String Bending

To a large extent, string bending is what makes guitar playing sound like guitar playing. It is one of the most important elements you need to master in order to make your playing sound professional. To control string bending, you must develop a close link between your "ear" and your fingers so you can bend consistently to the right pitch, not too high (sharp) or too low (flat). Of course, like most things, to get something out of it you have to put some work into it and this is no exception. So meet it head on. Persevere. Practice until the neighbors theaten to have you locked up! It may take some time, but eventually.you'll get it—and it will have been well worth the effort.

When a string is bent, its pitch goes up. Therefore, an up arrow indicates that a string is to be bent, and a number in parenthesis gives the target pitch. Keep in mind that you don't actually fret the string number in parenthesis, but rather, that number gives you the destination pitch, where the note *would* be found if it were played on that same string without a bend. For example, the following bend takes place entirely at the 7th fret. The "9" in parenthesis represents the pitch equivalent that your bend will reach. Since the bend raises the pitch two frets, this is a "two fret" bend, also known as a "whole step," or "full step" bend. Listen to the example and copy the way it sounds.

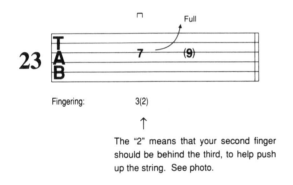

Fingering: 3(2)

↑

The "2" means that your second finger should be behind the third, to help push up the string. See photo.

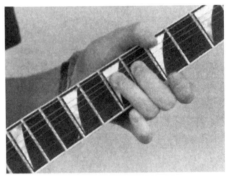

Full-step bend

If you are new to string bending, you probably had some difficulty knowing exactly how far to bend. To help get a better feel for this, play the second and third strings together in example 24 and bend until they sound the same. When they do, you are bending exactly one full-step because the note on the higher string is a full-step above the other note. (Specifically, the 9th fret, third string is the same pitch as the 5th fret, second string, and they're both a whole step above the 7th fret, third string.) Before you try it, listen to example 24 and notice how the turbulence between the notes stops as the bend reaches pitch. Playing two strings together like this is called a "double stop" bend.

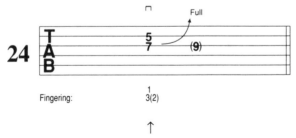

Fingering: 1
               3(2)

↑

This means that your 1st finger frets the note on the second string while your 3rd finger (with 2nd) takes the third string bend.

Now move these double stop bends up and down the neck:

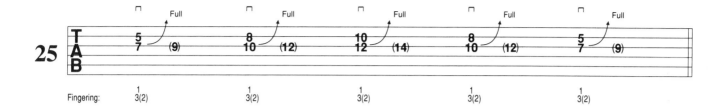

Example 26 uses a similar idea on the first and second strings. This time, instead of letting both strings ring together, see if you can get the right pitch by memory. Play the first note (which is the target pitch) and listen to it a moment. Then, continue to imagine (or hum) that pitch while you bend the other string up to it.

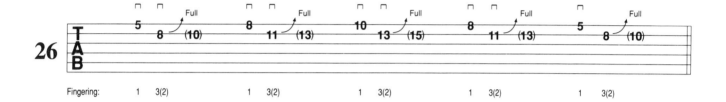

An arrow back down means to release a bend and return the string to its unbent position. *Do not lift up*, but rather, keep pressure down on it while you pull the string back to its unbent position. Avoid making noise on the other strings by using your muting techniques. (Which by this point you should have amazing control over!) Bend smoothly and try not to "pluck" the lower strings excessively as you release the bend.

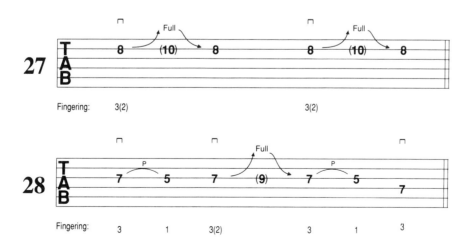

Sometimes a bend is not followed by a release, but by a note on a different string. In this case, don't release the bend until you're about to play the next note. Then, at the same time you go for the next note, release the bend quickly, lifting pressure off of the fretboard. If you do it right, you won't hear the release.

Obviously before a bent note can be bent up again, it must be released. But in the following example, the releases are so fast that you don't really hear them. Instead, you hear the repeated bend upward. Therefore, it is written without showing the releases.

Vibrato

Vibrato is a wavering of pitch, produced by repeatedly bending and releasing a string. It brings the notes to life, improving their sustain and helping to generate harmonic feedback. (See page 46 for more about sustain and feedback.)

To play a note with vibrato, press the side of your first finger against the neck of the guitar. Then, twist your wrist to pivot your hand as in the photos below. Although this is called *finger vibrato*, it's not so much a motion of the fingers as it is a motion of the wrist and forearm. (Of course your fingers move because they are attached to your hand and wrist.)

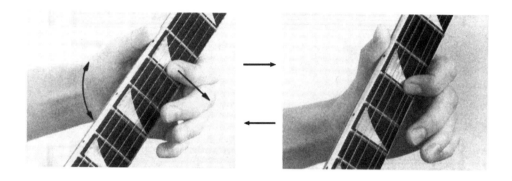

Practice the examples below with a slow vibrato on each note. It should be smooth and under control. On the first and second strings, push the string up to bend it instead of pulling it down. (That way you won't be pulling the strings off the fretboard.) The symbol ⌁⌁ indicates that a note should be played with vibrato. (As a general rule, any note that you hold out should be played with vibrato—unless it is moving up or down, as in a bend.)

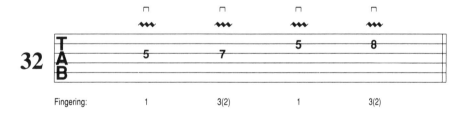

Metal Riffs

Short lead guitar phrases called "riffs" or "licks" usually involve string bending, hammer-ons and pull-offs. Below are several combinations that are commonly used as building blocks for longer phrases. Again, the examples are written in the low A minor pentatonic position, but practice them in the octave position as well. (On the tape or CD each example is played in both positions.) First, listen to each example to copy the timing of the notes "by ear."

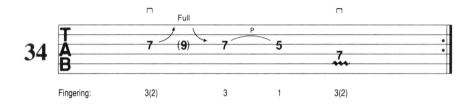

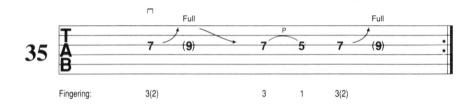

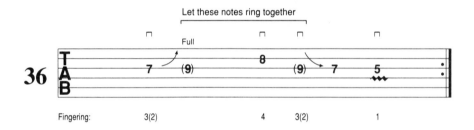

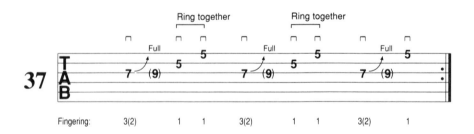

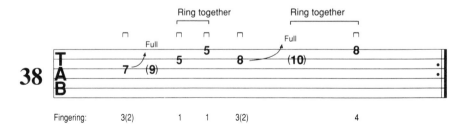

The riffs below are a little faster. If necessary, slow down a little until you get comfortable with them. Above all, make sure they sound good! The speed will come with time. Also, the symbols "/" and "\" mean to slide up or down the neck, respectively. Listen for these slides where they are notated in the following examples and notice the effect that they give.

39

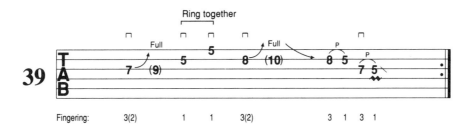

Fingering: 3(2)   1   1   3(2)   3 1 3 1

40

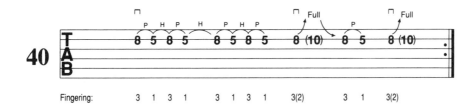

Fingering: 3 1 3 1   3 1 3 1   3(2)   3 1   3(2)

41

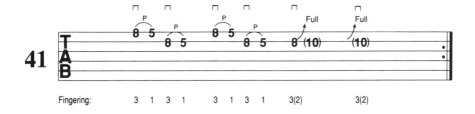

Fingering: 3 1 3 1   3 1 3 1   3(2)   3(2)

42

Fingering: 3 1 3   1   3 1 3 1   4   1

43

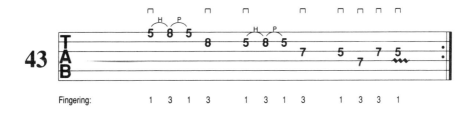

Fingering: 1 3 1 3   1 3 1 3   1 3 3 1

Metal Jam #1

Metal Jam #1 is a short tune with full band accompanyment in which you will play a "question/ answer" style solo with my pre-recorded lead track. There are three parts to this tune and they are labelled A, B, and C. (The structure of the whole song is ABC ABC AA-fadeout, with solos over the B and C parts each time.) To start the first solo, I come in with a short lead lick (the "question") followed by a pause of exactly the same length as that lick. During this space, you "answer" my riff. At first, just learn and repeat what I play—like an echo. (My riffs are written out below. Again, copy the timing "by ear.") After you've got that down, try throwing in different riffs. You can use some from the previous pages or improvise your own. (*Improvise* means to create licks on the spot as you play.) For the second solo, the sequence is reversed so you play the "questions" and I respond with the "answers."

Slow-Note Terror

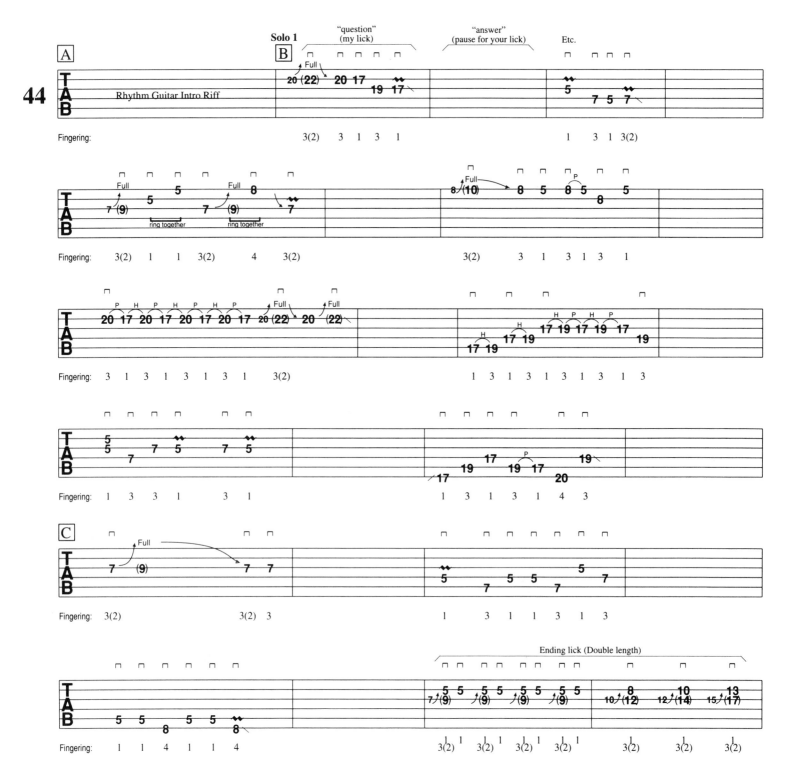

44

The rhythm guitar track is written out on page 42 in the appendix and the song is remixed without any lead guitar as example 91.

CHAPTER TWO

Rhythm Notation

Pitch is only one aspect of music. The other half of the story is *rhythm*—that is, when to play the notes and how long they last. Rhythm refers to the whole timing aspect of music. (Don't confuse this technical definition of rhythm with the common labelling of chording and soloing parts as "rhythm guitar" or "lead guitar" parts. In the technical sense, all notes have rhythm.) Neither rhythm nor pitch is more important than the other; they are simply different aspects of music, like two sides of the same coin.

If you have ever tapped your foot to a song (and I'm sure that you have), you know that there is a steady pulse that you can feel. This is called the *beat*, and it's the unit of time in music. Every note is measured in terms of the beat.

Usually, these beats are grouped together in fours, with an emphasis on the first beat of each group:

1 2 3 4 1 2 3 4

When the beats are grouped like this, the music is said to be in *4/4 time* (also called *common time*). The 4/4 symbol is called a *time signature*. Each group of four beats is called a measure, or bar, and is separated from the next measure by a bar line. A double bar indicates the end.

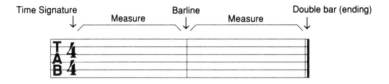

A *whole* note lasts for a whole measure, or four beats. *Half* notes last two beats. *Quarter* notes are one beat, *eighth* notes are a half beat (or, there are two eighth notes per beat), and *sixteenth* notes last a quarter of a beat (or, there are four sixteenth notes per beat). The pyramid diagram below shows the relative lengths of the notes.

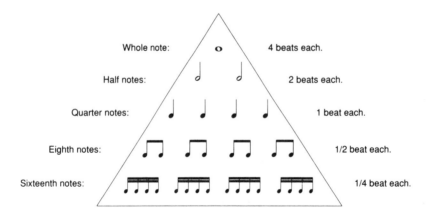

Sixteenth notes are twice as fast as eighth notes, eighths are twice as fast as quarters, etc. Keep in mind that this is only true if the speed, or tempo, is constant. To describe the actual speed of any particular notes, you need two things: The tempo (number of beats per minute) and the type of note (eighth notes, sixteenth notes, etc.).

In tablature, the note heads must be replaced with fret numbers. However, in all other respects the rhythm notation applied to tablature is exactly like that of normal music notation (staff). Listen to each example and follow along with the notation to get a feel for how it works. Then try playing along, tapping your foot with the beat and counting out loud. The counts of the beat are written below each exercise. (Before each exercise you will hear a four count intro to establish the tempo.)

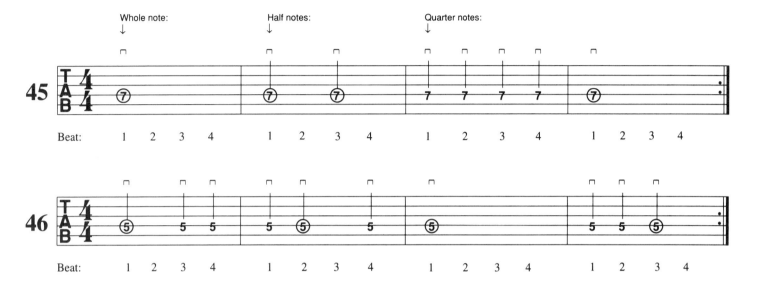

Eighth notes are one-half beat each. Another way of looking at it is that there are two eighths per beat. This subdivides each beat into "downbeats" (the first part of a beat, marked by the count itself) and "upbeats" (the halfway point between downbeats). As you tap your foot, you should clearly mark not only the downbeats, when your foot taps the floor, but also the exact timing of the upbeats by pausing with your foot in the air at the specific moment of each upbeat. Below, the upbeats are marked with the symbol "+". As you play along with these examples, count out loud: "one, and, two, and, three, and, four, and…"

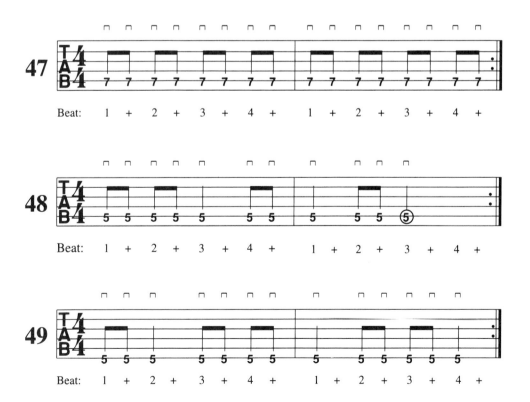

A *rest* is the musical term for a space with no sound. Stop the strings and hold them quiet for the length of the rest. The various types of rests are shown in the examples below. Also, note that a dot placed after a note adds 50% to the length of that note—therefore, a dotted half note lasts for *three* beats. Make sure you keep your count steady as you play.

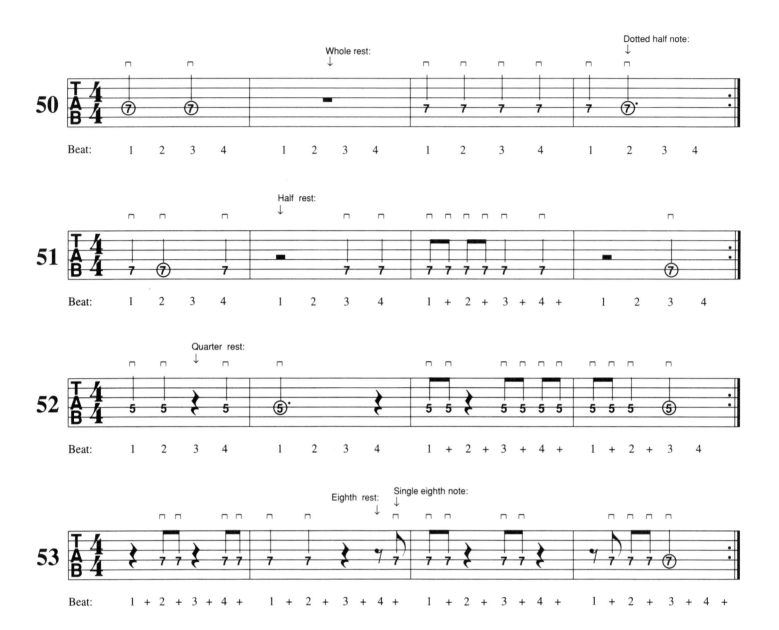

When notes are written on the higher strings, the stems will go down instead of up. This makes no difference in how they sound.

Below, rhythm notation is combined with simple lead melodies. Practice these lines along with a metronome to keep your count perfectly even. Also, notice that the last two notes in example 56 are both on the same fret. Don't lift up off of the fretboard to change strings or there will be a break between the notes. Rather, *roll* your third finger onto the higher string. To do this, make sure that you play the second to last note on your finger*tip*.

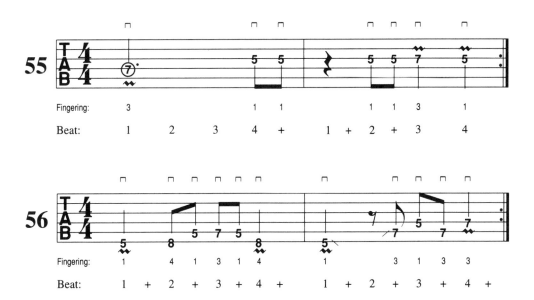

String bending gets a little more complicated with rhythm notation. Examples 57 and 58 both use the same notes, but they are applied to different rhythms. In example 57, the starting pitches and target pitches of the bends are all separate notes that fall on distinctly separate beats. In example 58 however, the string is bent up immediately so what you hear is really the pitch of "9" for the duration of the first note. Therefore, no note stem appears on the "7" and it is of a slightly reduced size. If this distinction seems confusing at first, listen to the examples and count along with them. When you hear the rhythms, it should all make sense.

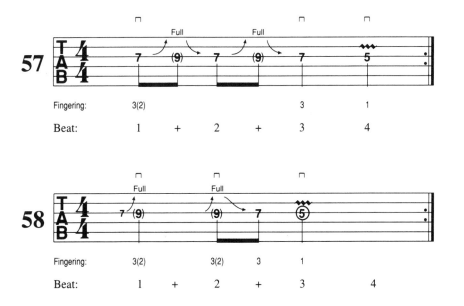

Syncopation

As you've already seen when you played eighth notes, some of them fell on the beat (or *downbeat*) and others fell on the "+" (or *upbeat*). When a note which falls on one of the "+'s" is held over into the following beat, the sounding rhythm temporarily "goes against" the natural pulse of beats. This effect is known as *syncopation*, and it is fundamental to many styles of music including rock and heavy metal.

In the following exercises, a *tie* (‿) is used to create syncopations. When you see a tie connecting two notes, pick the first note normally, but then let it ring through the duration of both itself and the note to which it is tied. In other words, a tie turns two notes into one note that rings from the beginning of the first note to the end of the second note. As you practice the following set of exercises, tap your foot along evenly with the metronome and notice how the sounding rhythm moves "against" the beat.

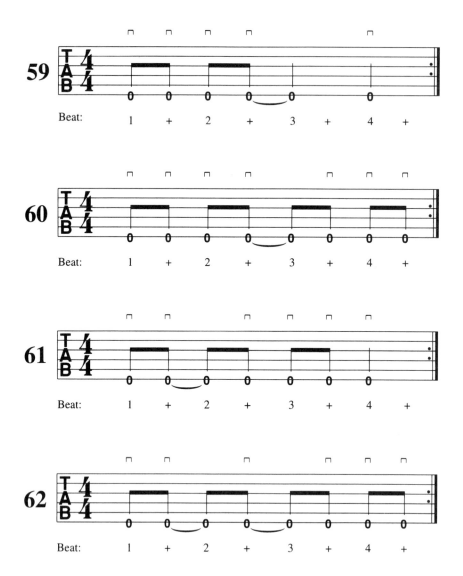

To play metal guitar well, you need to master syncopation. This can take some practice, so keep coming back to the exercises on this page until you've nailed them. The goal is to be able to feel and maintain a steady beat, even when the rhythm that you are playing moves against it. In other words, you are trying to feel two different rhythms at the same time—both the underlying beat and the sounding rhythm. *Therefore, if you aren't tapping your foot right, then you aren't practicing these exercises right.*

Example 63 demonstrates an alternate way to notate the following syncopation—substituting a quarter note for the two tied eighth notes. (Both are one full beat.) Notice that the rhythms of the first and second measures below sound identical.

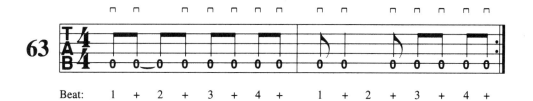

As you saw earlier, a dot placed after a half note increases its length by 50%, for a total of three beats. When a quarter note is dotted, its length is likewise increased by 50%, for a total of one and a half beats—the equivalent of a quarter note tied to a single eighth note. Notice that the rhythm in the first measure below sounds identical to the rhythm in the second measure.

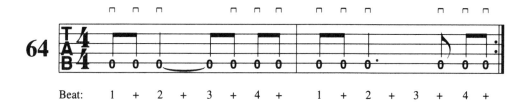

The following 2-bar riffs use syncopated rhythms. Remember to tap your foot evenly with the metronome.

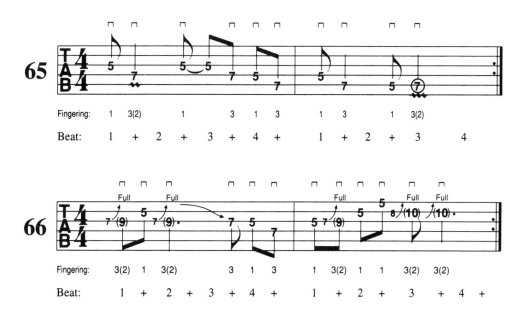

Sixteenth Notes

To play sixteenth notes, you will use "alternate picking." This means that the string is picked both on the downstroke and again when the pick is moving back up (the *upstroke*), enabling you to pick twice as fast without actually moving the pick any faster. The symbol " ∨ " indicates that a note is to be picked with an upstroke.

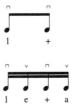

As you play example 67 count the sixteenths out loud: "one-e-and-ah, two-e-and-ah," etc.

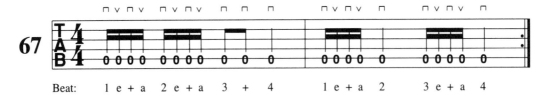

When sixteenth notes are combined with other note values within a single beat, the rhythmic figures look a little different. The first figure below consists of an eighth note on the downbeat followed by two sixteenths—I call it the "gallop" rhythm. The second one is simply the reverse of this, so I refer to it as the "reverse gallop." The last two figures utilize a dotted eighth note, which lasts 3/4 of a beat (or the length of three tied eight notes). No alternate picking is required, because the sixteenth notes are all played using hammers, pulls, and bends.

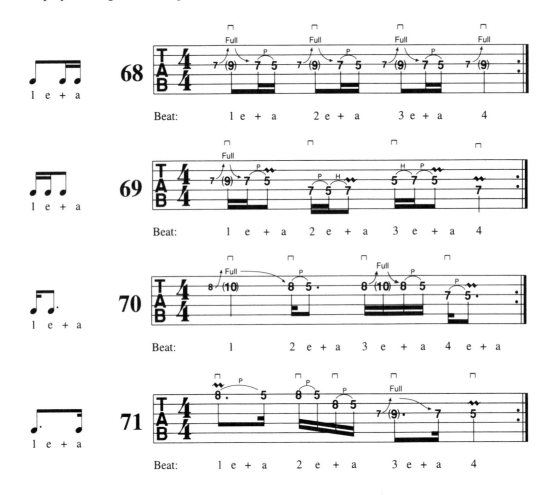

Triplets

A triplet is three notes evenly spaced in the time where there would normally be only two notes. The most common type of triplets are eighth note triplets, with three notes evenly spaced in one beat. The "3" above each figure in example 72 tells you that they are triplets.

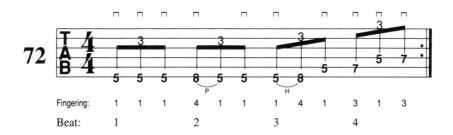

Example 73 switches between eight note triplets and other rhythmic divisions. Listen first, to get a feel for it.

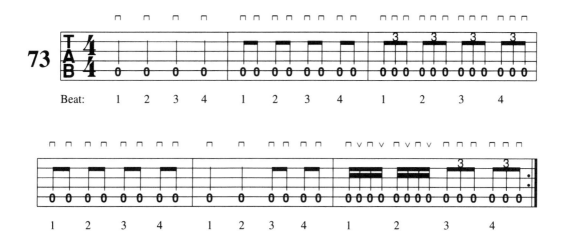

Quarter note triplets are three notes spaced evenly over two beats, and are more difficult to play well. Listen to the staggered-feeling rhythm in example 74 and copy the way it sounds.

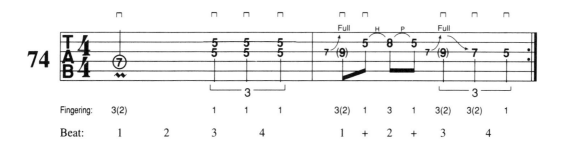

Nothing will make you learn rhythm notation faster than actually trying to write it out. So now, go back in chapter one to examples 11-22 (in the section "Hammer-ons and Pull-offs") and examples 34-43 (in "Metal Riffs"), listen to each one again and write in the correct rhythm notation. Then write in the notation for the licks in "Slow-Note Terror." If you have trouble with this, find someone to help to you—but don't skip it! When you are finished, go on to the next page.

Palm Muting

This muting, or "muffling" technique is used often in metal guitar. When played with a distorted sound, palm muting gives notes a strong and aggressive "crunch" (from the pick striking the string) followed by a deeper, "bassy" tone that rings for a short duration. (Don't confuse this technique with the other type of string muting, in which excess string noise is eliminated. Although they are both called "muting," they are separate techniques which produce different results.)

To play notes with a palm mute, lay your right hand palm lightly over the ends of the strings as in the photo below. For a tighter mute (less ringing of the strings), move your palm a little in the direction of the neck so that more of the strings are covered. If you want the strings to ring more, move your palm the other way (toward the bridge). Exactly how much of the string you should cover depends on the sound that you want. If you are playing with a heavy sound, you will probably want to mute tighter, but if you have a weaker, less-distorted sound you will want to mute a little less. Listen, and make your own judgements as to what works best with your sound. In any case, don't press down on the strings too hard or the pitch of the notes will go up.

Muting with the Right Hand Palm

Palm muting is indicated by the symbol "P.M." Listen for the characteristic "crunch" of the muted notes in example 75. In number 76, some of the notes are muted while others are not. Make sure that you cover the strings with your palm for the muted notes, but lift up and entirely off of the strings for the unmuted notes. If you are doing it right, the unmuted notes will stand out as accents.

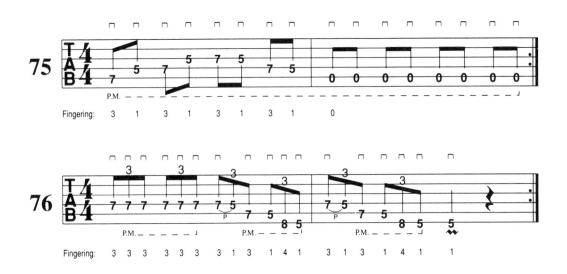

Staccato

Staccato is a musical term that means a note is to be played very short and not allowed to ring on for it's full length. (Use both hands to stop the strings.) The symbol for staccato is a dot placed directly over or under a note. Although notes played with palm muting are also shortened, that isn't the same thing as playing with staccato technique—staccato notes are short, but they are *not* muted.

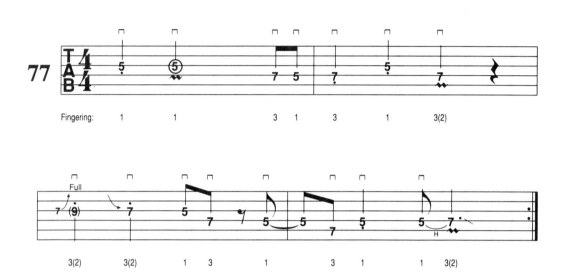

Example 78 shows a riff that uses both staccato and palm muting techniques. Notice the difference in the sound produced by these two techniques.

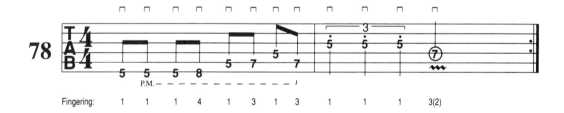

Vibrato on a String Bend

To play vibrato on a bent note, first bend the string up to pitch, then release the bend slightly, followed by another slight bend up, release, etc., over and over. For the first exercise below, try making a least four bends and releases, making sure that each bend reaches the correct pitch.

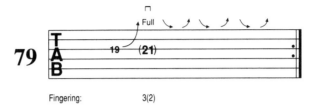

When you speed up the bends in the previous exercise slightly, you are playing a slow vibrato, as in the next example.

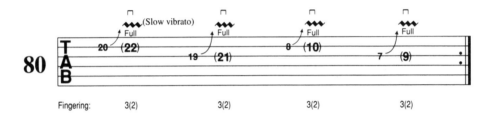

Vibrato can be slow or fast, and wide or narrow, depending on what you feel fits the music best. The riffs in examples 81 and 82 use a slightly faster vibrato, but remember—control and evenness are more important than speed at this point. Only do it as fast as you can do it well.

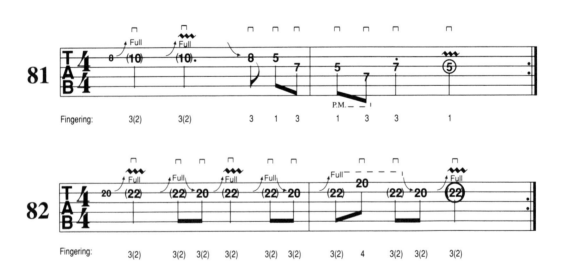

36

Microtone Bends

Sometimes a slight bend is given at the tail end of a note to give it a "bluesier" kind of sound. These bends are called microtone bends because they don't raise the pitch of the string even one full fret. Instead, these bends are written as being a 1/4 step bend, which equals the pitch of only one half of one fret.

In reality though, you don't have to worry about exactly how far you bend these notes. No specific target pitch is given because it doesn't really matter—the pitches your ear perceives are the *unbent* notes. This is because the bend occurs toward the end of the sounding note, so you don't really hear it as a note with a raised pitch but rather as a subtle effect which makes the notes come alive. Listen to them first, and then make your bends sound the same way. For the bends in example 83 below, pull the string down with your first finger instead of pushing up.

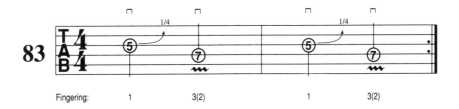

Pay close attention to the microtone bends of staccato notes in riff 84, below. The second measure introduces a note that is not from the minor pentatonic scale. However, since it is sandwiched in between the other notes and not accented, it acts as a sort of "filler" or "melodic lubricant," and it doesn't change to melody of the riff very much. Notes used in this manner are called *passing tones*. The last notes in the riff below show an alternate way to play the two lowest-sounding notes of the A minor pentatonic scale.

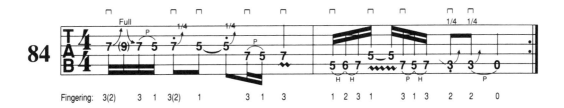

Playing in Other Keys

So far, all of the riffs in this book have been in the key of "A," meaning that in each case the "A" note has been the tonal center, or "home base." (Technically, the note that names a key is called the *keynote*.) Any note may act as this central pitch, making it being possible to play in any of twelve different tonal centers, or "keys." To play the minor pentatonic scale in different keys, you simply slide the entire pattern up or down the neck of the guitar so as to match the root of the scale pattern with the new keynote.

The following fretboard diagrams demonstrate the minor pentatonic scale in several different keys: A, B, D, E and F#. (A sharp sign (#) raises the pitch of a note one fret, so F# would be located on the second fret, 6th string—one fret higher than F.) Notice that in each case the scale pattern's lowest root (represented by a square) corresponds to the keynote. For example, the "A" note is located at the 5th and 17th frets, so that's where the A minor pentatonic scale pattern begins; the "B" note is located at the 7th and 19th frets, so that's where the B minor pentatonic pattern begins; "D" is at the 10th fret; "E" is at the 0 and 12th frets; etc. (If you don't remember the names of the notes on the sixth string, go back to page 8 and review them now.)

Underneath each diagram is the same two-bar riff, except that it is moved, or *transposed* into each key. Also, the riff introduces *pickup notes*, which are notes that precede the first full measure of the phrase. In this case, since they are two sixteenths—a total of one half of a beat—they come in on the "+" of 4. (You count backwards for pickup notes. For example, if there are three eighth notes as pickups, you would play them as the last three eighth notes of the countoff measure: "+ 4 +".) The riff is written only in the low position each time, but play it in both.

A minor pentatonic

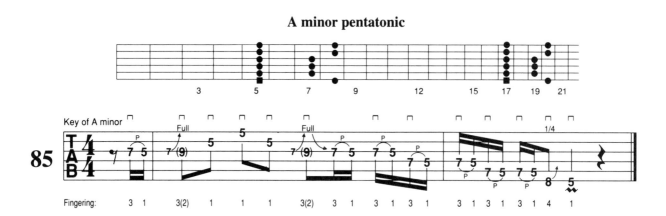

B minor pentatonic

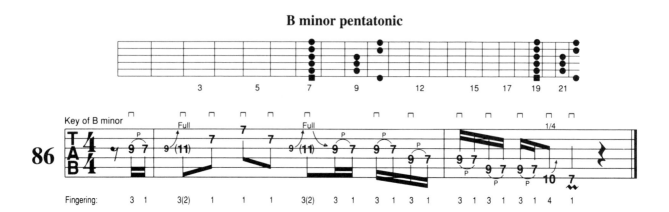

D minor pentatonic

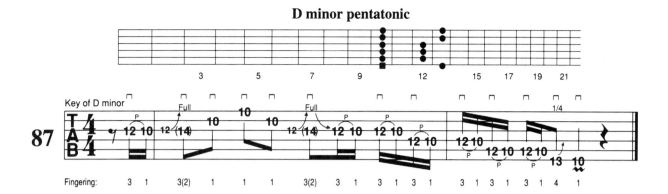

E minor pentatonic

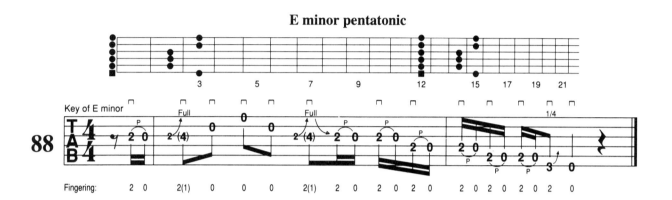

F# minor pentatonic

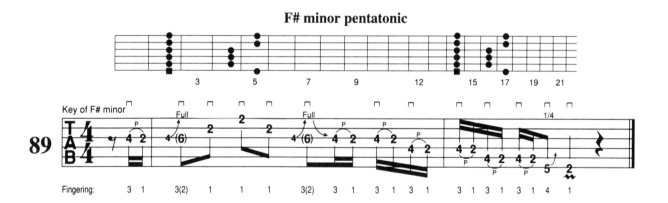

Usually, chord progressions remain in one key, so all you have to do is stay in the right scale and everything will sound OK. You do not have to change with each chord. For example, "Slow-Note Terror" is in the key of A minor throughout, although the chord progression is AAGD (for part A) ACGA ACGD (for part B) and GACD GACE (for part C), with one measure per chord and some connecting riffs. Since all of these notes are in A minor, it will sound fine to solo in the A minor pentatonic scale throughout the entire song.

If, however, the music moves to a particular chord and stays on it for a long time, you have a key change and you must move the scale pattern accordingly. For example, in "Mistakes?!? Off With Their Heads!!!" on the next page, the first riff is in the key of A. Then, when the solo begins, the progression moves up and hovers around B for 8 bars, after which it continues through a cycle of key changes before finally returning again to A.

Before you go on to that solo, go back through all the riffs you have learned in this chapter and practice them in at least four different keys. Even though you will be playing the same relative patterns, the different positions will be a little different. You should be equally comfortable playing in *any* key.

Metal Jam #2

Metal Jam #2 features some more "question/answer" style soloing, but this time the licks are two bars each instead of one, as in "Slow-Note Terror." The song structure for "Mistakes?!?" is AB AB AA-fadeout, with solos over the B sections. Pay attention to the key changes! Again, just repeat my licks at first, then after you've got that down, throw in different variations. In the second solo, the sequence is reversed so that you take the "questions" and I respond with the "answers." So tear it up! But remember—*no mistakes,* or the guitar police may be knocking at *your* door!

Mistakes?!? Off With Their Heads!!!

RHYTHM GUITAR TRACKS

For those of you who just have to learn *everything*, here are the rhythm guitar parts for "Slow-Note Terror" and "Mistakes?!?" Both tunes are remixed without the lead guitar as examples 91 and 92 so you can hear the rhythm guitar part more easily. You can also use these tracks to practice soloing by yourself—without "trading licks" with the pre-recorded lead track—or, you can trade riffs with another guitarist.

Slow-Note Terror

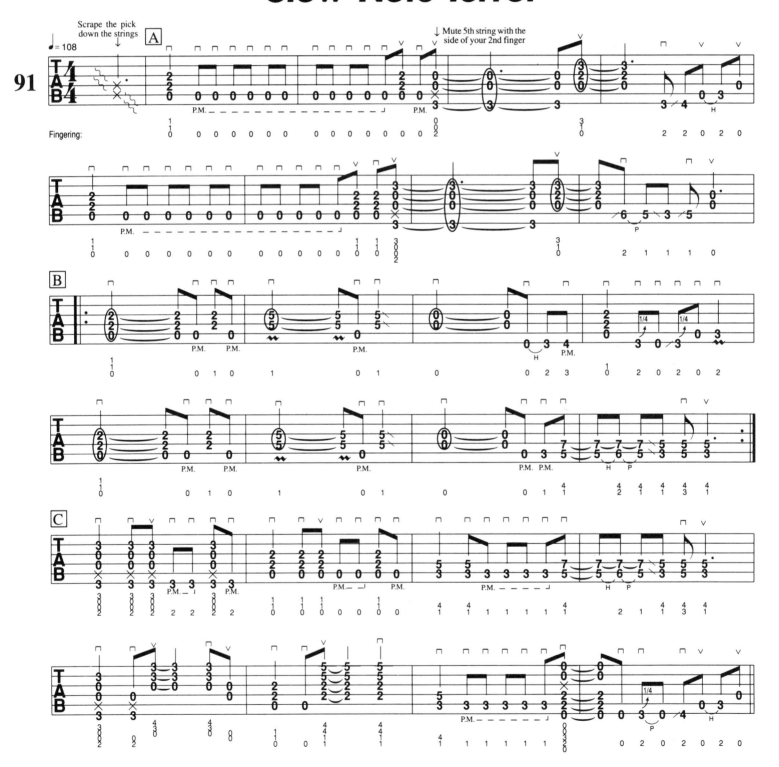

Repeat sections A, B, C, A, A (until fade-out)

Mistakes?!?
Off With Their Heads!!!

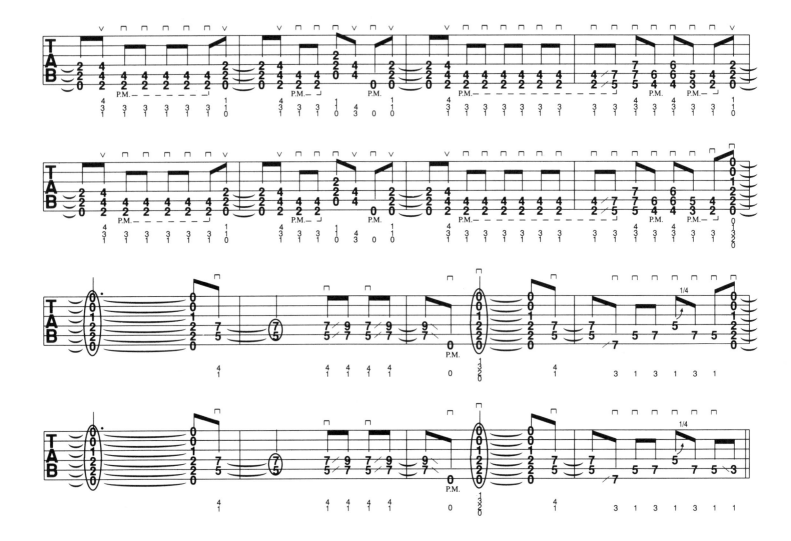

Then repeat sections A, B, A, A (until fade-out)

Now you are ready to start **Metal Lead Guitar, Volumes One** and **Two,** which feature twelve full solos that become progressively more advanced with each passing chapter. And if you haven't already begun **Metal Rhythm Guitar, Volumes One** and **Two,** it is recommended that you do so at this point. The rhythm side of things complements the lead books, and completes the picture. In addition, a number of other books supplement these core methods, including *Speed Mechanics for Lead Guitar, Metal Guitar Tricks, Thrash Guitar Method,* and *Secrets to Writing Killer Metal Songs.* See the inside back cover for more information.

GETTING THE SOUND

A great guitar sound makes the simplest riffs sound great. While different metal players may have slightly different guitar sounds, the characteristic lead guitar sound is basically a heavily distorted sound, with soaring sustain. To the "dry" sound, effects are often added to enhance the sound, give it depth, or create other special sounds. Each element of the system is discussed below.

Distortion

Distortion is also known as "overdrive," " gain," " clipping," "fuzz," or a "dirty" sound. Whatever the name, it is caused by amplifying a signal beyond the circuit's ability to faithfully reproduce that signal. Since this traditionally takes place in the amplifier, obviously the amp is one of the most important factors in producing a good metal sound.

Today, most guitar amps achieve distortion by using two amplifier stages. In the first stage, the signal is amplified until distortion occurs. Then the second stage amplifies that distorted sound to the desired listening level. With this setup you don't need high-volume to achieve distortion as in the "old days" (i.e., the ancient times before 1970). These two amplifier stages are labelled "pre" and "post" gains, "gain" and "volume," "volume" and "master," or some combination of these. For a distorted sound, turn the volume control on your guitar all the way up, turn the first gain level on your amp all the way up to 10, and then bring the second stage up to the appropriate listening level, as shown below. On the other hand, a "clean," or undistorted sound is made by making sure that neither stage is overdriven.

93 Demonstration of the difference between a *clean* and *distorted* sound.

A device known as a "distortion pedal" will add, in effect, another stage of gain. (It is called a pedal because it is placed on the floor and operated by foot.) There are a number of distortion or overdrive pedals to choose from, all claiming to offer the best distortion. Although they produce slightly different qualities of distortion, in reality it's impossible to say that any are better than the others. What sounds good with one amp setup won't sound good with another, so you just have to follow your ear and make whatever control adjustments are necessary. These pedals typically offer control over the amount of distortion, the output level, and some type of "tone" control to adjust the relative amount of bass/treble in the sound, which brings us to the next subject: EQ.

EQ

The term *equalization*, or EQ for short, refers to the frequencies that make up a sound. On most amps the EQ consists of three tone controls labelled bass, middle, and treble, which can be used to make the sound deeper (more "bassy") or brighter (more "trebly"), etc. There are also "EQ pedals" that can further and more accurately shape your sound. (Since the single tone knob on your guitar simply "rolls off"—or decreases—the high frequencies, metal players generally leave it on 10.) The following listening example will help to familiarize you with the character of these different frequency bands.

94 Demonstration of several different EQ settings:
   a) A thick "bassy" tone—bass up, treble down
   b) A thin "trebly" tone—treble up, bass down
   c) A "mid-boosted" tone—middle up, bass and treble flat (that means "0")
   d) A mid-scooped tone—middle down, bass/treble up (common in thrash metal)

The Guitar

Many factors influence the sound of the guitar itself, including the type and density of wood from which it is made, any routed cavities, the type of "pickups" and where they are located, the material and design of the bridge, and even the kind of strings and whether they are new or old—but for our purposes, the pickups are probably the most important single factor.

Pickups come in single coil and double coil varieties. Double coil, or *humbucking* pickups, are essentially two single coil pickups side by side, and so are twice the size. However, more recently they have been designed to fit into the space of a single coil—stacked on top of each other or crammed tightly side by side. In any case, double coil pickups generally produce a stronger signal than single coil pickups. This will help to overdrive the amp more, and give you a heavier distortion. But don't get the idea that you must have the highest output pickup available. There are many ways to boost output, and the highest output pickups may not have the best-sounding tone for you.

Pickups positioned near the bridge give a brighter sound, while those in the neck position will sound deeper. The traditional lead sound uses only the bridge pickup—also called the "lead" pickup. In fact, some guitars are equipped with only this one pickup. Most guitars, however, have at least a bridge and neck pickup, or sometimes a third pickup in between those two. (On the recording that accompanies this book, I used only the lead pickup.)

Sustain and Feedback

Good "sustain" is an important part of a great lead sound. It means that the notes will ring on longer, instead of dying away quickly. On its own, the guitar actually has very little sustain—when you pluck a string, there is a sharp attack and then the note fades away quickly. But when it is amplified and distorted, sustain increases dramatically. When the note is loud (at first), the strong signal just overdrives the first amplifier stage, creating more distortion—not more volume. (Remember that the second amplifier stage controls the volume level.) As the note fades, the "thickness" of distortion drops somewhat, but the volume remains at very nearly the same level as when the note was struck. (Sustain!) Still, however, the note will eventually die out.

With the help of high volume, though, you can achieve infinite sustain—that is, as long as you hold a note it will continue to ring. This can occur because of something called the *feedback loop.*

As you know, a loud guitar can make things vibrate and rattle. Suppose the low E string is picked. The soundwaves travel through the air and if another guitar is nearby, the vibration will cause its E strings to also begin vibrating. This is called *sympathetic vibration.* Now, this sympathetic vibration will also cause the E string to ring on the guitar that you are playing, assuming that it is in the room as well. But since it's plugged in, the more the string rings, the more sound comes out of the amp, which keeps the string ringing, etc. An infinite loop has been created. Usually a higher harmonic of the original note dominates and the low E turns slowly into "feedback." Because of this, it is sometimes referred to as "harmonic feedback." Jimi Hendrix first put it to use in the late 60's, and it has been used by metal players ever since.

95 Demonstration of "feedback."

A smooth finger vibrato will help to sustain notes, and when combined with high volume, can generate harmonic feedback. However, harmonic feedback can be elusive because the high gain and volume levels necessary can also cause unwanted "microphonic feedback"—an annoying high-pitched squealing. Finding the right balance can be difficult (not to mention a little hard on the ears), so if you're as nuts about it I am, you can check out a device called the Sustainiac® Sustainer. It creates a "soundless" feedback loop and makes obtaining feedback a cinch at any volume, and it can be turned on and off with the flip of a switch. (I use one of these.)

Effects Devices

There are also several "effects," including delay, reverb, flange, and chorus, that may be used to further enhance the sound. These devices may be in the form of "pedals" or rackmount units.

Delay is an echo effect, repeating the sounds you've just played. The number of repetitions as well as the time period between repetitions is adjustable. In the following examples, the abbreviation "ms" stands for milliseconds and means "thousandths of a second."

96 a) Here is a tight delay—set for one repeat at 100ms.
b) Here is a longer, "slapback" delay—set for one repeat at 400ms.
c) Here is a longer delay set for several repeats at 500ms.

Reverb is similar to delay but instead of a distinct echo, reverb gives the effect of a room sound where the echoes are diffused and indistinct. The following examples use different reverb settings.

97 a) Here is a "large hall" reverb
b) Here is a normal-sized room reverb
c) Here is a combination of reverb and delay

Flanging and *chorusing* are produced by combining a very tight delay (10-40ms) with pitch shifting—that is, changing the pitch of the incoming signal. When this effected signal is combined with the "dry," unaffected signal, flanging and chorusing result.

98 a) Here is a typical "flanged" sound
b) Here is a typical "chorused" sound
c) Here is a combination of flanging, reverb, and delay.

Concerning the order in which you run the effects, distortion should be first, followed by the other effects—otherwise, you will be distorting the effects instead of applying the effects to a distorted guitar sound. If your amp has an effects loop, try using it for any delay, reverb, flange or chorus effects. That way, they won't be distorted in the amp's first gain stage.

Some units, particularly the rackmountable ones, combine several or all of these effects with distortion, compression, and EQ. In addition, many of these units are programmable. This means that you could have one patch with no distortion (clean), compression, short delay and chorus, another with distortion, long delay and reverb, and switch between these two sounds at the touch of a button. Also, these units open up the possibility of having things like chorused reverb, reverb on the repeats of the delay, and other interesting combinations. These units are more expensive than a single pedal, but in the long run they are cheaper (you are buying all the effects together), not to mention better sound quality and lot more control with less cords and confusion.

In conclusion, a guitar sound is a very complex interaction of many elements. You just have to experiment to find what you like and what works for you. While all of these toys can be a lot of fun (and they are worth investigating), don't forget about the most important part of your sound—you! What comes out of your speakers is a combination of both your setup and your technique.

My Setup For The Recording

On this recording, as is common practice in the studio, the guitar was set up without any pedals except distortion, and the speaker cabinet was miked. Then, to this "dry" or, "uneffected" sound, a slight delay and reverb were added with the studio's signal processors to give it some depth. I played a Jackson Soloist guitar equipped with a Sustainiac® GA-2 Sustainer and a Seymour Duncan Custom pickup. This was run through a Boss distortion pedal (PD-1), into a mid-70s Marshall 100 watt amp head, and then into a Marshall 4x12 speaker cabinet. The effects unit used was an Alesis Quadraverb, which is a rackmountable multi-effects unit.

HOW TO PRACTICE

First of all, you should have your practice area set up so that everything you need is within reach and easily accessible. Keep your guitar out of its case and on a guitar stand, so it is a constant reminder for you to practice. Then you can pick it up and play whenever you have a few minutes, without having to go through the hassle of getting it out, setting it up, and putting it away again. Your amp controls should be within reach, as well as your metronome, any music books you are using, and the controls to your cassette or CD player. Make it comfortable—you need a stool or chair (without arms!), and a music stand for your books.

When people ask me how much they should practice, I usually answer with the question: "Well, how good do you want to be?" You should practice as much as you can, and as long as you are inspired to practice. The key is that you have to enjoy it, or you'll burn out and tire of it long before you've seen the improvement that you want. If you really must have a specific amount of time to shoot for, start with *at least* an hour or more each day and see how fast you are improving. Also, it's generally better to play for a while, take a short break, and then come back to it rather than doing practice "marathons," but everyone is different and you just have to find out what works best for you.

Since music is best taught by example, you should definitely be learning the songs and solos that inspire you. But you shouldn't *only* be learning songs. You also need to understand the principles and techniques that you are using and you need to acquire a knowledge of music. Ideally you want to be a good musician, not just a good guitar player. For that reason, the books in this series are designed to cover the elements of music as well as the specific techniques. Go through them and learn everything you can, but don't stop there! Get transcription folios of your favorite bands, put on their CDs, and learn everything! Get together with friends and play the stuff. Get a band together and play—rehearsing with a band will teach you things that you wouldn't learn just by practicing alone in your bedroom.

As far as working out of books, I'm often asked by guitarists if it's OK to work from several books at the same time, or if it's better to finish one book before starting another. Concerning my books at least, I believe that you're better off using several together at the same time, because many skills and techniques overlap somewhat from one book to another and you can benefit by seeing the different approaches. (Each of my books focuses on a different aspect of guitar playing.) Also, and probably most importantly, practicing a variety of material keeps you from getting burned out on any one thing. Just don't become so scattered that you don't *finish* each book. Along the same lines, many people are under the mistaken notion that you must first master rhythm guitar before you can begin lead—*not true*. While rhythm guitar is generally easier than lead, that is not always so, and furthermore the line between them is not always clear cut—"rhythm" guitar parts often include riffs that seem suspiciously lead-like. In reality, notes are notes; it's just that some are faster and more difficult to play than others. And the bottom line is that you should be practicing music that is just slightly beyond your ability, regardless of whether it is considered "rhythm" or "lead" guitar. You can and should learn both simultaneously.

And finally, on the issue of taking guitar lessons: There is no doubt that a good teacher can help you learn a lot faster by showing you the right way to do things and avoiding bad habits. Also, there is no substitute for having another more experienced player point things out that you may not be aware of. The important question is, how do you know if a teacher is good? Ideally, you should learn from someone who specializes in the style(s) you like, because a person who is really accomplished at a particular style is likely to know a lot more about the ins and outs of that style than someone who isn't. (Some teachers may claim to teach styles in which they really aren't competent because they're in the business of giving lessons, so don't be afraid to ask the questions that are important to you.) On the other hand, good players don't always make good teachers, so ask around about their reputation. If you are *really* serious about music, check into some of the music schools around the country that have programs for the styles of electric guitar in which you are interested. Musician's Institute in Hollywood, California, is probably the best known, but there are many other schools that offer similar programs. So, until we meet again in the next book—have fun with your playing, and good luck!